BLAST OFF!

ALL ABOUT SPACE MISSIONS

Miriam Gross

PowerKiDS press™

New York

Published in 2009 by The Rosen Publishing Group, Inc.
29 East 21st Street, New York, NY 10010

First Edition

Editor: Joanne Randolph
Book Design: Greg Tucker
Photo Researcher: Jessica Gerweck

Photo Credits: Cover © NASA/Age Fotostock; p. 5 © Stocktrek Images/Getty Images; pp. 7, 17 © Time & Life Pictures/Getty Images; p. 9 © National Geographic/Getty Images; pp. 11, 13 © Getty Images; p. 15 © Haag + Kropp/Age Fotostock; p. 19 © NASA/Getty Images; p. 21 © spacephotos.com/Age Fotostock.

Library of Congress Cataloging-in-Publication Data
Gross, Miriam J.
  All about space missions / Miriam Gross. — 1st ed.
      p. cm. — (Blast off!)
  Includes bibliographical references and index.
  ISBN 978-1-4358-2740-0 (library binding) — ISBN 978-1-4358-3138-4 (pbk.)
ISBN 978-1-4358-3144-5 (6-pack).
  1. Astronautics—Juvenile literature. 2. Outer Space—Exploration—Juvenile literature. 3. Space probes—Juvenile literature. 4. Space flights—Juvenile literature. I. Title.
  TL793.G78187 2009
  629.4'1—dc22
                                        2008032837

Manufactured in the United States of America

CONTENTS

A trip into space is called a space mission. Space missions can take minutes or even years. Some missions are carried out to launch **satellites**, or send them up into space. Others send up tools to build space stations. Many missions explore, or find out more about, outer space.

Space missions teach us about the world we live in and about the **universe** around us. Space missions may bring pieces of other **planets** back to Earth. These discoveries can give us knowledge of how our world formed.

This astronaut spent 5 hours on a space walk to work on a satellite called the ISS.
His mission was to add parts to the ISS and fix parts already in place.

In order to make sure that spaceflight was safe for people, **scientists** first sent animals up in rockets. The first living things to make the trip into space were fruitflies in 1947. Two years later, a monkey named Albert II launched into space, followed by a mouse in 1950.

These animals shot up in rockets, but they did not reach high enough to **orbit** Earth. The first living creature to orbit Earth was a dog, named Laika, who traveled in the Russian satellite, *Sputnik 2*. In 1961, a chimpanzee named Ham tried out the spacecraft that would soon launch the first U.S. **astronauts** into space.

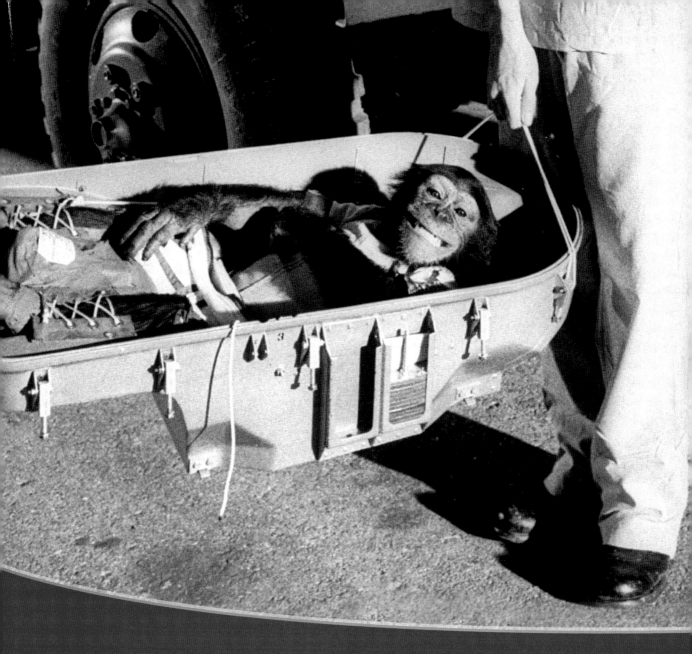

Ham has just come back from his test mission in this photo. His flight was an important step on the way to human spaceflight.

In 1958, the United States formed a special department for space exploration. It was called the National Aeronautics and Space Administration, or NASA, and its first job was to try to send people into space. NASA chose seven men to be the first American astronauts. The astronauts were part of a **program** called Mercury, which was named after the spacecraft that would carry them into space.

The Mercury program flew six missions. The first Mercury mission sent Alan Shepard into space on a Redstone rocket. In the third Mercury mission, John Glenn orbited Earth. America was now on its way to exploring outer space.

This is a Mercury mission space capsule that is on its way down after a test flight in July 1960. The manned flights in the Mercury program were flown between 1961 and 1963.

On July 16, 1969, three astronauts blasted into space aboard *Apollo 11*. Their names were Neil Armstrong, Buzz Aldrin, and Michael Collins. They would soon become the most famous astronauts in history.

Apollo 11 was a mission to the Moon. The astronauts reached the Moon in three days. Neil Armstrong was the first person to step down onto the Moon. The astronauts planted a U.S. flag and collected rocks to bring back for study. The next day, they came back home to Earth. In all, there were six Apollo missions that landed on the Moon.

Here John Irwin is shown in front of *Apollo 15* and the American flag during the fourth Moon landing. There were nine Apollo missions to the Moon, with six landings.

Some space missions can be carried out without sending people into space. Using unmanned spacecraft called probes, scientists can learn all about places in the universe that are too far away for people to reach.

Some probes fly near other planets and send data, or facts, back to Earth. These probes take pictures and measure things such as **temperature**. Other probes orbit planets. Some probes can even land on the planets. They can bring back matter, such as dirt or rocks, for scientists to study on Earth.

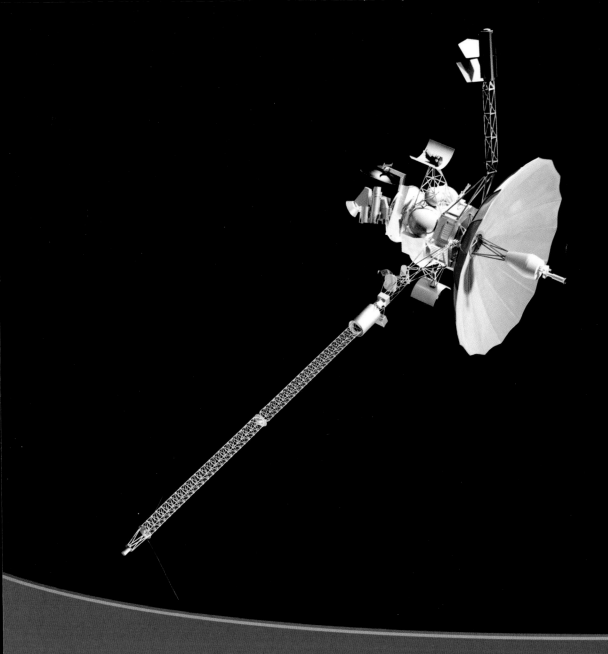

This is the *Galileo* probe, which was launched in 1989 to study Jupiter. *Galileo* orbited Jupiter for 14 years, sending back photos and data to scientists on Earth.

NASA sent its first probe to Mars in 1964. Scientists are interested in Mars because there may once have been life there.

The *Mars Odyssey* probe launched in 2001. It orbits Mars and sends pictures back to Earth. The *Mars Odyssey* has helped scientists map Mars. It also found signs of underground ice on Mars.

In 2004, NASA sent two rovers, named *Spirit* and *Opportunity*, to land on Mars. Rovers are robots that roll over the surface of a planet, taking pictures and studying things like rocks and soil. The Mars rovers are looking for more signs of water so scientists can study where the water came from. In 2008, another rover, named *Phoenix*, landed on Mars.

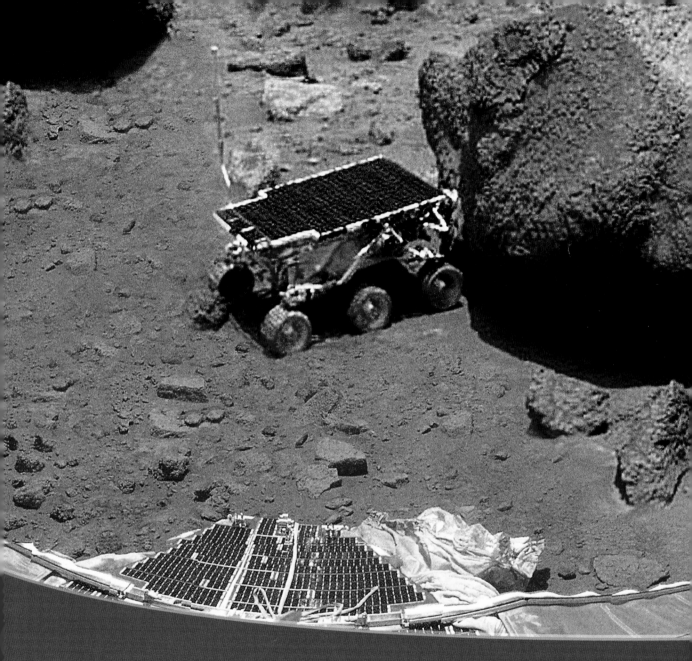

This is the *Sojourner* rover, which was sent to Mars as part of the Pathfinder mission in 1996. The rover was meant to send back data that would help later rovers have successful missions.

In 1977, NASA sent two probes, called *Voyager I* and *Voyager II*, to explore the planets Jupiter and Saturn. The probes discovered that there were **volcanoes** on one of Jupiter's moons. They also sent back pictures of Saturn's rings.

Scientists learned so much from the Voyagers' missions that they sent them beyond Jupiter and Saturn. The Voyagers explored Uranus and Neptune, the farthest planets from the Sun in the **solar system**. Over 30 years later, the Voyager probes are still exploring outer space.

This close-up photo of Saturn and two of its moons was taken by the *Voyager 1* probe. The probe found out that Saturn's rings are made up of thousands of rings of ice and other matter.

In 1997, NASA worked with the European Space Agency and the Italian Space Agency to launch a special mission to Saturn. A spacecraft, called *Cassini*, would orbit the planet. A probe, called *Huygens*, would explore Titan, one of Saturn's moons.

In 2004, after seven years of traveling, *Cassini* reached Saturn's orbit. *Cassini* had traveled 3.5 billion miles (6 billion km)! Several months later, the *Huygens* probe landed on Titan. *Cassini* has taken close pictures of the golden rings of rock and ice that circle Saturn. It also found that there could be life on one of Saturn's moons.

Here the *Cassini* orbiter blasts off for Saturn aboard a powerful rocket in October 1997. *Cassini* carried the *Huygens* probe inside.

In 1990, the **space shuttle** *Discovery* launched the *Ulysses* solar probe into space. A solar probe explores the Sun. *Ulysses* was named for an **ancient** Greek hero who took a long journey. The *Ulysses* solar probe traveled over 6 billion miles (10 billion km).

Ulysses orbited the Sun for about 18 years. It studied the hot wind that comes from the Sun. It also studied matter in solar storms, among other things. Though there were no astronauts on this mission, some 200 scientists played a part. They worked on understanding the facts that the probe sent to Earth.

Here workers check *Ulysses* to make sure it is ready for launch. The big, dishlike shape you see here is the part that would send data about the Sun back to Earth.

There will continue to be space missions as long as there are places to explore in outer space. The Voyager probes keep traveling farther out into the universe.

Scientists will make better probes so we can learn even more about other planets. Probes may one day be able to dive under the water on one of Jupiter's moons.

People will also explore new places and travel farther into space than ever before. NASA plans to send astronauts back to the Moon and then to Mars. Each space mission will bring us more knowledge about our universe.

GLOSSARY

ANCIENT (AYN-chent) Very old, from a long time ago.

ASTRONAUTS (AS-truh-nots) People who are trained to travel in outer space.

ORBIT (OR-bit) To travel in a circular path around an object.

PLANETS (PLA-nets) Large objects, such as Earth, that move around the Sun.

PROGRAM (PROH-gram) A plan for doing something.

SATELLITES (SA-tih-lyts) Spacecraft and natural objects that circle Earth.

SCIENTISTS (SY-un-tists) People who study the world.

SOLAR SYSTEM (SOH-ler SIS-tem) A group of planets that circles a star.

SPACE SHUTTLE (SPAYS SHUH-tul) A reusable spacecraft made to carry people and goods to and from space.

TEMPERATURE (TEM-pur-cher) How hot or cold something is.

UNIVERSE (YOO-nih-vers) All of space.

VOLCANOES (vol-KAY-nohz) Openings in planets that sometimes shoot up hot melted rock called lava.

INDEX

WEB SITES

Due to the changing nature of Internet links, PowerKids Press has developed an online list of Web sites related to the subject of this book. This site is updated regularly. Please use this link to access the list:
www.powerkidslinks.com/blastoff/missions/